RUNNING

**Everything You Ever Wanted to Know About Running
That Your Books, Magazines and Coaches Never Told You
but Your Body, Bank Account and Ego Always Did**

by JIM RAMSAY

ILLUSTRATIONS BY BOB CRAM

A FIRESIDE BOOK
Published by Simon & Schuster, Inc.
NEW YORK

A Fireside Book
Published by Simon & Schuster, Inc.
Simon & Schuster Building
Rockefeller Center
1230 Avenue of the Americas
New York, New York 10020

FIRESIDE and colophon are registered trademarks
of Simon & Schuster, Inc.

Designed by Stan Drate/Folio Graphics Co. Inc.

Manufactured in the United States of America

Printed and bound by Fortune Litho

10 9 8 7 6 5 4 3 2 1

ISBN: 0-671-53068-2

*This slim, lanky, long-muscled book
is for my mother,
Juanita Ramey Ramsay,
who, although not responsible for its content,
can be held accountable for sharing with the author
her blazing intellect
and instilling in him
a well-conditioned sense of whimsy.*

Achilles tendon

A

accelerate

(1) Increase your foot speed on a running course. (2) Increase the speed of your car in an attempt to run down the jogger who made an impolite gesture toward you at the last stoplight. (3) Add a celery garnish to a Bloody Mary as your reward for running around the block once and only stopping three times to catch your breath.

Achilles tendon

tendon connecting the calf muscle to the bone in the heel of the foot. When Achilles—the famous runner and warrior-hero of Homer's *Iliad*—was a baby, his sea-nymph mother dipped him into the River Styx to protect him from all injury. She held him by the heel, however, and Achilles was subsequently killed by an arrow that struck him in that vulnerable place. The Achilles tendon has been vulnerable to injury in all runners ever since Achilles' mother made this stupid mistake. A fact usually not reported is that she also held him by the toes, feet, ankles, shins, calves, knees, groin, thighs and back.

acrylic fleece

sales technique in sporting goods stores where prices are tripled for ultra-light running equipment. When you are a fat customer who thinks that this more expensive gear will make you look thinner, the technique is known as "cellulite."

adrenalin stimulating hormone produced by a runner's endocrine system as a response either to the thrill of competition or in anticipation of a tax audit.

aerobics (1) A form of indoor, bad-weather exercise in which runners jump around while keeping time to a Michael Jackson record in an attempt to show their lungs and circulatory system who's the boss and convince those organs that they had better shape up, or it's no more cholesterol and cigarettes for a week. (2) An orderly line of cheap ballpoint pens used for notations in running logs.

arch support sarcastic encouragement, e.g., "Sure I'll pay your entrance fee and watch you run. I need a good laugh."

arthroscopy minor surgery that middle-aged runners arrange to have performed in early spring, providing them with an excuse to sit and watch baseball for the remainder of the running season in air-conditioned bars—hence the literal translation of "arthroscopy" from the Greek, "joint viewing."

athletic supporter philanthropist who makes a strapping donation to a running scholarship.

autosuggestion advice runners doing roadwork give to the driver of the car that nearly kills them, usually taking the form of, "Hey, haircake, why don't you take your car and shove it up your exhaust pipe!"

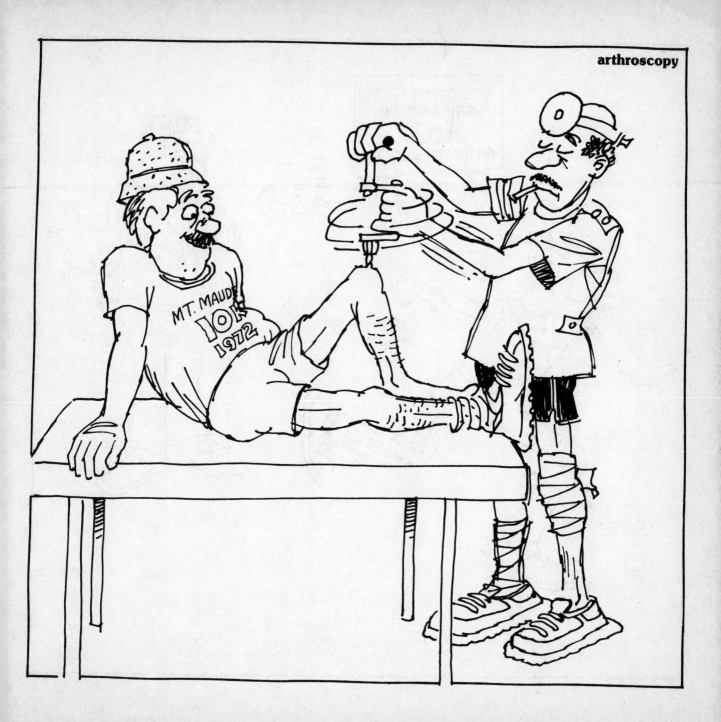

balance

B

balance   (1) Correct dynamic positioning of the runner's body in three-dimensional space to achieve most efficient running form that expends the least amount of energy. Balance is a subtle, tricky quality, and poor balance can frequently be corrected only with expensive equipment, attire and coaching. (2) The trivial amount of money remaining in a runner's bank account after purchasing expensive equipment, attire and coaching.

balls of the feet   inaccurate reference to the anatomy of male runners; also called "metatarsal macho."

bank   (1) Degree to which a running track's curves are raised on the outside to counter the centrifugal force of a runner rounding the curve. (2) Financial institution, usually in Switzerland, where world-class amateur runners deposit, in numbered accounts, corporate recognition of their love of the sport.

baton   a tube-shaped wooden stick with design characteristics that make it become impossibly small, slippery and invisible when one relay runner attempts to pass it to a teammate.

baton hand-off   attention-getting headline on a sign posted by the CIA around the U.S. Olympic track team's equipment room, warning foreign agents to keep their hands off and further stating that violators will be prosecuted for attempting to apply grease, glue or other foreign substances to the U.S. relay team's batons. Baton hand-off should not be confused with the "baton exchange," which is a highly specialized commodities market in Pasadena, California, that trades in relay race, twirling and orchestra conductors' batons used in Olympic festivities.

beginner   someone who says, "I'm going to skip all this preliminary hoo-hah and just jump right into a marathon."

blood pressure   the pressure you receive from your relatives to please stop all this running and go out and get the birthday presents you promised them.

blood vessels   boat-shaped containers filled with blood, e.g., a marathoner's running shoes after the 22-mile mark.

bone chips   calcium-rich runner's snack invented by the Mexican butcher/long-distance runner Dorito Sanchez.

Boston Marathon   world famous long-distance event founded by Paul Revere. Revere, a silversmith, devised the competition in order to corner the concession on winner's trophies. He originally conceived of the marathon as an Anglo-American horse race to be held at night. Because of complaints from Bostonians who did not want their sleep disturbed, the starting gun was replaced by a lantern in the Old North Church. The crafty Revere signed up undernourished Tarahumara Indians as jockeys in order to gain a low-weight advantage, and instructed them to signal any gains made by the foreign

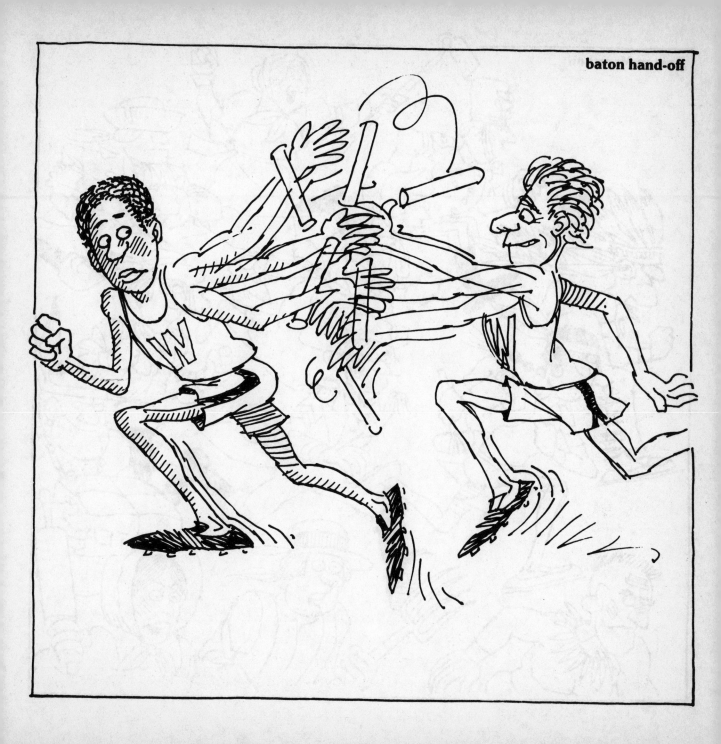

Boston Marathon

competition by shouting, "The British are coming, the British are coming!" The Brits, however, withdrew their horses from the competition at the last minute because of sour grapes over repeated defeats in the America's Cup boat race, and Revere was forced to change the event to a footrace against British Redcoats. The Indians won handily and later celebrated their victory by throwing the post-race tea party supplies into Boston Harbor, a historic act known as the "splash heard 'round the world."

breath

generic term for runner's cycle of oxygen-carbon dioxide exchange. More specific terms include "pant," "gasp," "wheeze" and "death rattle."

burn out

a sly technique that middle-aged runners use to get out of the summer marathon they foolishly committed themselves to while drinking too many beers with running cronies after work. Typically, such runners purposely lie out in the sun for eight hours on the day before the marathon, get a second-degree sunburn, call their friends and cancel, and then lie in a hammock the day of the race while their spouses bring them cool drinks and gently rub Noxzema on the affected areas while saying, "Here, you poor dear, this will get the burn out."

C

calcaneus (1) Injury-prone heel bone that runners frequently cushion with a padded heel cup. (2) Newsletter distributed to runners by a dog food manufacturer.

calf portion of the back of the leg between the knee and the ankle, so termed because after running it tends to feel like it has been roped, tied and branded.

calorie unit of heat energy used to calculate the balance between energy expenditure and nutritional intake. For example, one mile equals two small pretzels; five miles equals an apple; twenty-six miles equals a tuna salad (hold the bread and mayo); and if you run one hundred miles a day, you can have a dish of Frusen-Glädjé chocolate/ chocolate chip whenever you want.

carbohydrate loading the procession of dock workers in Naples, Italy, who carry huge sacks of spaghetti, linguini, fusilli and lasagna to waiting cargo vessels to be shipped to America and eaten by millions of would-be marathon runners who, after the meal, decide to have another bottle of chianti and forget the whole thing.

cardiogram a singing telegram for middle-aged runners who overdo it and have to go into the hospital for bypass surgery.

Charlie Horse

cardiovascular fitness	the degree to which the cardigans belonging to a runner who graduated from Vassar still fit her.
Central Park	running practice area in New York City where personal best times can be dramatically improved because of the city's thoughtful provision of vehicle bans, joggers' lanes and muggers.
Chariots of Fire	a 15-minute film short on running that was stretched to feature length by the addition of 2 hours of slow-motion running footage.
Charlie Horse	famous American Indian runner of the late eighteenth century who won all races against U.S. Cavalry competition by kicking opponents in the calves.
cheetah	(1) Graceful feline predator often used as a symbol of speed. (2) Any participant in an urban marathon who sneaks onto the subway during a competition, rides for several miles, then sneaks back onto the course again.
chest pains	a symptom indicating that one is either running or dying.
cinder track	memorial track surface created by the International Olympic Committee, composed of the last remains of Olympic-opening-ceremony torchbearers who screw up on the last two steps as they are about to light the Eternal Olympic Flame.
cold weather running	a form of exercise requiring support undergarments to prevent chafing and injury, underpants, thermal underwear, one pair of thin socks, one pair of heavy socks,

running shoes, sweat pants, nylon warm-up pants, leg warmers, a T-shirt, a sweat shirt with a hood, a nylon windbreaker with a hood, a wool hat, earmuffs, a ski mask and gloves. The runner is now equipped to stand immobilized for long periods of time in bitter weather. Running is out of the question.

Communist bloc countries   any country in which starting blocks are decorated with hammers and sickles and runners are called to these blocks with the phrase, "Runners take your Marx. . . ."

competitive   what you are when you elbow the runners crowding you, step on the heels of those in front of you, or don't move aside for runners behind you on a narrow track. (See *"unsportsmanlike."*)

conditioning   the sum of activities runners use to increase their feeling of well-being. These activities include salivation over scantily-clad runners of the opposite sex ("Pavlovian" or "bare conditioning"), cool-down exercises ("air conditioning") and proper grooming ("hair conditioning").

contact sport   any of several sports requiring violent contact, e.g., football, ice hockey, la crosse or the beginning of any marathon receiving national television network coverage.

cool-down exercises   smoking a cigarette after sexual fulfillment; drinking beer from a frosted mug; taking a dip in the ocean; sipping a tall, iced gin and tonic; turning on the air conditioning; and other similar activities used to avoid actually running. (See *"warm-up exercises."*)

Corrida del Toros	(Spanish, "Running of the Bulls.") Noontime exercise program developed in city financial districts for out-of-shape stockbrokers.
cross-country run	long-distance track event routed through churches and cemeteries. Also called a "steeple-chase" or "pall-vault."

D

das boot	German-made, high-cut running shoe for extremely wet running conditions. Comes with optional periscope and torpedoes to slow the competition.
decathlon	cathene-free race for runners who can't sleep.
dedication	cancelling a free lunch date at an expensive restaurant, returning an erroneous liquor store delivery and passing up the opportunity to meet Tom Selleck or Christy Brinkley in order to run in the Swamp and Sand Marathon.
dehydration	condition dangerous to the health of runners, resulting from fluid loss through perspiration. Many older runners have the sense to avoid the problem by constantly consuming large quantities of beer and eliminating running from their lives entirely.

delinquents	teenage joggers who pass you easily when they should be doing their homework.
diathermy	therapeutic heat treatments for sore running muscles. Physicians who specialize in such treatments use the fees thus obtained to pay for their own solar diathermy in the Caribbean.
dig down	(1) To reach for one's reserves by ignoring pain in an attempt to improve performance. (2) To go into one's savings account in order to come up with the bucks for the latest line of running gear. (3) To provide a 6-foot deep opening in the ground for overweight, middle-aged executives who decide to skip the after-dinner cigar and knock off a few miles instead.
dope test	quiz used to sort out stupid runners from those of average intelligence. Questions included in the examination are, "What distance did Roger Bannister have to cover to break the 4-minute mile?" "What city hosts the Boston Marathon?" and "What is your name?"
draft	(1) To follow closely in the "wind shadow" of the runner in front of you so as to reduce your own wind resistance. Lead runners who pick up the pace to avoid providing this advantage to those behind them are termed "draft resistors." (2) "draught"—unit of measure of high-carbohydrate liquids consumed by runners before marathons and, indeed, before practically everything else. (See "bruise," def. #2.)

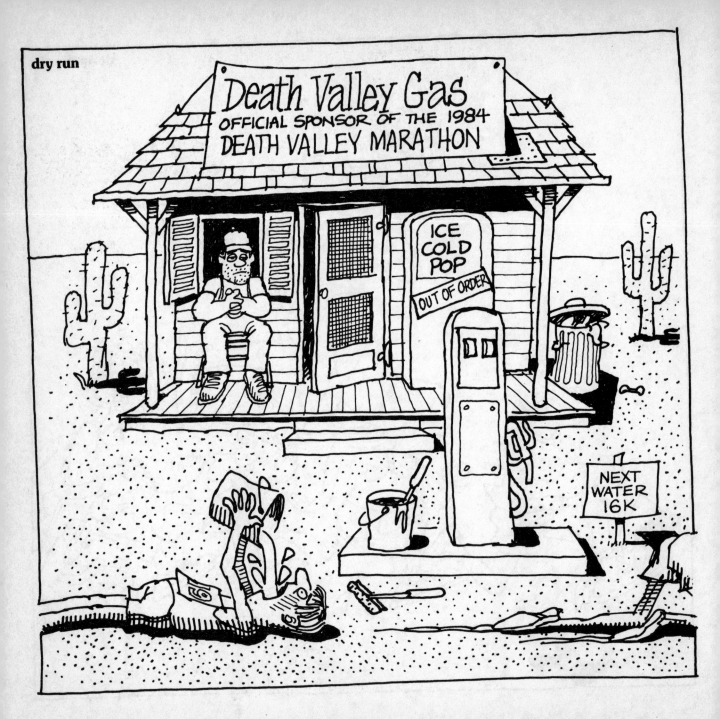

drag
(1) Anyone who says, "Look, let's forget the drinks and partying and make it an early night so we can get in an extra 10 miles tomorrow before breakfast." (2) Wind resistance encountered by male runners who choose to wear jogging bras, lace panties, sequined tank tops and high-heeled running shoes.

dry run
(1) The Death Valley Marathon. (2) Any marathon in which the water-station volunteers abandon their posts to pursue frivolous activities like playing video games. (See "laps.")

E

EEG
("electroencephalogram") A tracing of brain waves indicating electrical activity in the runner's brain. A typical runner's EEG is indicated below.

effete
feet requiring the widest running-shoe size.

Effingham
(1) Town in Central Illinois. (2) Substitute expletive used when the ligament attaching muscles from the

back of the thigh to the back of the knee is injured, as in, "There goes my effing hamstring again!"

egocentric   a runner who, after tripping over a baby carriage and knocking it down, says to the distraught mother, "Hey, it's okay, don't worry, I only lost maybe three, four seconds."

E.T.   (1) Elapsed time. (2) Nickname of a mysterious entrant in the 1984 Summer Olympics whose registered time for the 1500-meter run was 3.14159265 zartaks.

exhaust   *v.* Expend all available energy in a practice run or a competition. *n.* Invigorating cloud of gases provided for lead marathoners by television and film trucks, timer vehicles and motorcycle escorts.

F

Falmouth Road Race   combination road race and swearing competition that is traditionally started with the phrase, "Runners, to your bleeping marks, get set you bleeper-bleeping bleeps, go!"

fartlek   playful group wind sprints in which it is advisable to be the lead runner.

fascia strains   (1) Undue stress runners put on sheets of connective tissue that cover or bind together bodily structures; e.g., what happens to your stomach when you decide to

postpone your evening jog and finish off the second six-pack instead. (2) Runner's injury named after the railroad system in Italy that ran on time under Mussolini.

fast-twitch muscle fibers — structural component of sprinting muscles first discovered in material used in skirts worn by Tahitian dancers.

finish line — a come-on to members of the opposite sex by Finnish runners, usually taking the form of, "Hey, baby, you're yust about the cutest little reindeer I'm seeink here. After the race, let's you and me stop by my place for a sauna and a quick roll in the snow?"

finishing kick — state of euphoria experienced by runners who, in off hours, do furniture restoration and breathe in the fumes of glue, paint remover and lacquer.

fleet-footed — runner who is wearing boating shoes.

Frank Shorter — diet device used by runners to trim the fat, ugly, puckered little ends off hot dogs.

G

galavant — (French) The woman running in front of you.

gale — any wind in a runner's face. (See "zephyr.")

gambit　condition of legs when running through swampy, mosquito-infested areas.

gauge　to estimate distance, e.g., meters between you and runner in front of you, miles to the finish line or blocks to the outdoor cafe where you spend your time when your friends and family think you are out running.

gaunt　the typical appearance of a world-class runner. "gauntlet"—world-class runner who is under 10 years old.

gear shift　quick change of clothing, for example, when you start to put on the same sweaty T-shirt you've been running in for the last ten days, but see an attractive member of the opposite sex jog past and quickly change to a fresh, sexy tank top with "I Did It in the Bahamas" blazoned across the chest.

Geoff Smith　ex-firefighter from Liverpool, England, who won the 1984 Boston Marathon on April 16 in 2 hours, 10 minutes and 34 seconds—1 minute and 43 seconds off the course record set by Alberto Salazar in 1982. Smith's success has been attributed to years of geogging, avoiding sugar-laden spreads like geams and geollies, drinking plenty of fruity geuice, and setting a blistering, geot-propelled pace at the beginning of the race. After crossing the finish line, Geoff geustifiably geumpped for geoy.

glow　Victorian term for female perspiration, the proper use of which was emphasized by the phrase, "Horses sweat, men perspire and ladies glow." In today's more

liberated running vocabulary, everybody sweats, particularly the members of the General Motors Jogging Club when they attend to the details.

gonadotrophic of or relating to trophies given at macho running events such as the Iraqi Minefield Marathon and the Mount St. Helens "First-one-off-the-north-slope-before-it-blows-is-a-chicken" 10-K run.

gothic arch warm-up exercise in which the runner places a book on the floor, stands in front of it, then bends over backward and reads 100 pages. Titles of acceptable books for this exercise include *Dark Castle of Desire, The Master of Bloodmoor Manor* and *Selena's Storm-tossed Destiny.*

grade (1) Slope of a running surface, so named because of runners who, accustomed to flat courses, find themselves on a severe up-hill for the first time and cry, "Grade God Almighty!" (2) Academic mark that relates running to age, as in "F" for forty-ish.

Graham Greene snack crackers you forgot at the bottom of your running equipment bag 4 months ago.

gravity boots subjective feeling of any running footwear worn on a run of 10K or more.

groin pull rather unsophisticated come-on by a runner of the opposite sex.

gross national product spit, sweat and other equally unenchanting by-products that runners deposit next to the highways and byways of the nation.

H

haberdasher runner who enters dash events simply to sell running clothes to other competitors, usually by whispering unflattering comments at the start or finish line like, "Where did you get those baggy shorts? If I were you, I'd take them in a little here and here, or maybe you'd like to see something in a nice rayon?"

hale (archaic) Free of defect, disease or infirmity. This term is not applicable to anyone involved in running.

hammock make derisive comments about the size of a runner's haunches. Synonym used exclusively for female runners is "harass."

harrier (1) Cross-country runner. (2) What you become if you get into steroids.

Harvard Step Test test given by the Harvard Athletic Department to runners who want to enter that prestigious university, consisting of one question: "What *steps* have your parents taken to increase Harvard's endowment fund?"

Hermes (Greek myth) Son of Zeus and Maia, patron god of runners known as "messenger of the gods" because of his great speed, winged heels and hat, and ability to deliver flowers.

Hill

Hades; the Netherworld; the setting for Dante's *Inferno,* which has a sign over the entrance that warns, "All hope abandon ye who enter here!" Hill is a recurring religious, philosophical, moral and literary image, as evidenced by the following quotations, which all runners should commit to memory.

"Each of us bears his own Hill." (Virgil, *The Aeneid*)

"To appreciate Heaven well
'Tis good for a man to have some fifteen minutes of Hill." (Will Carleton)

"Hill is paved with good intentions."
(John Ray, *Proverbs*)

"Into the jaws of death
Into the mouth of Hill
Rode the six-hundred."
(Tennyson, *The Charge of the Light Brigade*)

"War is Hill." (William Tecumseh Sherman)

"Give 'em Hill, Harry!"
(supporter of Harry S. Truman)

"Hill is for Heroes." (title of a war film)

hill-training

important instruction middle-aged runners give each other consisting of the basic rule, "Avoid hills at all cost."

homestretch	indoor exercise performed in a runner's domicile consisting of standing on the toes and reaching for the bags of Twinkies, potato chips and chocolate fudge cookies hidden on the top shelf in the kitchen.
horny	(1) Adjective describing increase in skin thickness on runner's feet due to constant friction with footwear. (2) Adjective describing increase in runner's libido due to constant observation of those cute little shorts worn by runners of the opposite sex.
hospital	popular nationwide string of social clubs where runners hang out, lie about their personal best times and sign each other's foot casts.
humiliation	basic emotion felt by all runners who are outsprinted to the finish line by anyone else who is younger, older, fatter or thinner than they are.
hurdle	barrier placed in a runner's path that is designed to be surmounted regardless of the sacrifice, as in a coach saying, "No pain, no gain. The hurt'll be good for you."
hyperextended knee	injury sustained by any runner foolish enough to imitate the positions demonstrated by the instructor of a health club yoga class.

I

ice age

the age—usually in the middle forties—at which a runner decides to have one more bourbon on ice before setting out on a 2-mile run and then needs ice packs on feet, knees and head for a week after the exercise.

iliotibial band syndrome

this painful injury, known to sophisticated runners as "ITB syndrome," is caused by inflammation of the tendonlike band running from the hip to just below the knee. It provides the perfect excuse not to run since it can't be detected by X-rays. A perfectly healthy runner can thus say, "Sorry, I can't make it today because my ITB syndrome is acting up," and get total sympathy from those who mistakenly understand the phrase to mean a wasting disease of the lungs. The runner can then spend time pursuing more interesting activities like off-track betting (OTB syndrome), cashing in blue-chip communications stocks (ITT syndrome) or going to bed (GTB syndrome).

impact

(1) Collision of sole of running shoe with running surface that is transferred directly from foot to jaw, producing impacted molars. (2) Phrase used by runners attending out-of-town running competitions, as in, "Dear, do you have your shoes and warm-up suit?" "Yes, darling, I'm packed."

incompatible
income received by world-class runners for endorsing running gear, breakfast cereal, credit cards and whatever else their agents can dig up. The term derives from the fact that the checks received for such endorsements are so large that the runners in question are frequently seen fondling and patting them.

inconsistent
term you apply to a competitor who beats you by a hundred yards on one occasion and a mile on another.

indoor track
a completely covered track with a climate-controlled environment in which the 50-yard dash requires runners to negotiate three or more curves.

infinite patience
quality demonstrated by someone at a cocktail party who listens without complaint to a young man who has just (a) become the father of twins, (b) bought the latest edition of Trivial Pursuit and (c) finished third in his first organized 10K running competition.

inspiration/ expiration
brief sequence of events that begins when an overweight executive, watching a marathon on TV, is inspired to get out of the barcalounger and run swiftly around the block to see if the old legs are still in shape, and ends when the runner expires due to cardiac arrest. When a police photographer records the position of the body of deceased, the defunct runner is said to have had a "photo finish."

Iron Man Contest
an exhausting competition with non-stop, sequential events in long-distance swimming, bicycling and running. The title of the contest derives from the fact that

participants willing to subject their bodies to this kind of punishment possess unusually high concentrations of iron between their ears.

Isaiah 40:31	the source of the quote, "They shall run, and not be weary. . . ." We have to assume that the marathon was established after Isaiah's time.

J

jog	a large, stupid athlete.
jogging	the second gait of anthropoidal bipeds developed through evolutionary natural selection as a response to large carnivores, mudslides, pursuit of the opposite sex and as an activity that permits shoe and apparel manufacturers, orthopedic surgeons and podiatrists to make large amounts of money. Jogging is now believed to have first appeared in Pithsuntananthropus, an apelike creature who dwelt on the margins of the great forests of primeval Siberia. From there, members of the species jogged steadily eastward, crossed the land bridge at the Bering Straits, trotted southward and settled in

what is now California where they invented hot tubs, volley ball and avocado salad.

jog itch	desire to be intimate with a large, stupid athlete.
jog-and-kick	competitive running style in which you set a slow pace until another runner tries to pass you, at which point you crush your competitor's rib cage with a whirling "bite of the dragon" kung-fu move.

K

Kant	also known as the "categorical imperative," this term, named after the famous German philosopher, is the one you use when you've got a hangover and your running partner says, "Let's do another 5Ks."
kink	(1) Muscle soreness, usually in the neck, shoulders, back, thighs or calves. (2) Any of several sexual fetishes including liaisons that require running spikes, Nautilus machines or adhesive tape.
knee	a part of the body with such profound design deficiencies that Ralph Nader wants all years and all models immediately recalled.

knee

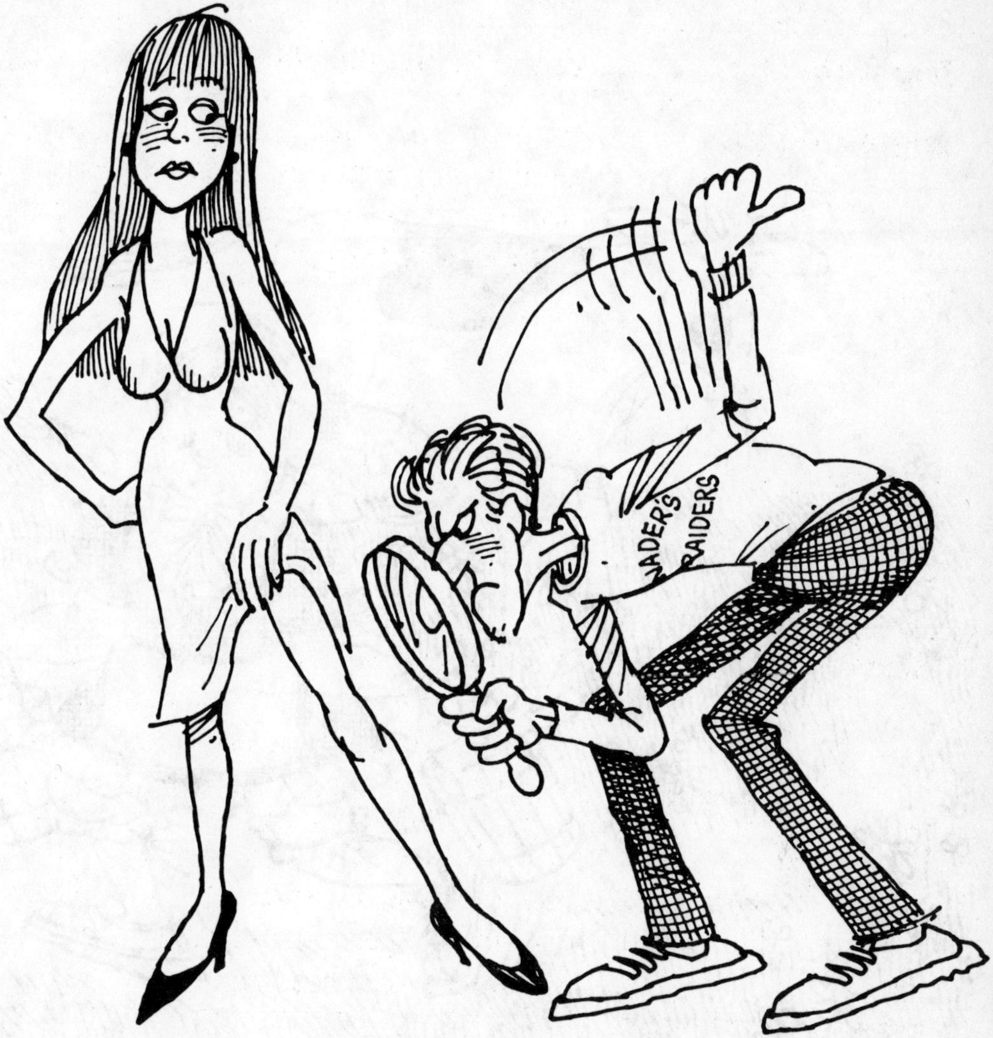

L

lapidary   jog around a milk-producing establishment.

laps   intake of liquid from mud puddles by marathoners when the water-station volunteers are goofing off.

leg cramps   a condition in the leg muscles achieved either through running or peak sexual activity. So why run?

long distance runner   anyone who is thin enough, in good enough condition and stupid enough to keep running after everyone else has quit.

L.S.D.   *Long Slow Distance.* A running schedule used exclusively by runners who jog along wearing mirrored sunglasses and look at their hands while saying, "Wow, it's like all shiny and I can see every hair." Sometimes the slowness is further accentuated, as when the runner stops for three hours to stare at gravel and can be overheard to mumble things like, "It's all here, it's all one, we're all gravel."

lunge   (1) To throw one's body across the finish tape in a desperate attempt to win. (2) The meal a runner has after breakfast and before dinner.

M

maintain contact

(1) Strategy by which you do not permit the lead runner to get so far in front of you that you cannot make up the distance. (2) Strategy by which you do not permit the cute runner you've followed for an entire marathon to wander away from the finishing area without getting a phone number.

marathon

the prolonged, strenuous activity with mares in which the thoroughbred racehorse Devil's Bag will be involved after his multimillion-dollar breeding syndicate puts him out to stud.

metacarpal

(1) Pertaining to the second joint of a runner's fingers, important in making victory sign after winning race. (2) Encountered a group of commuter-joggers sharing an auto to save gas.

meter maid

(1) A very short female runner. (2) A female runner of any height who runs very short distances.

middle distance

distance that increases in direct proportion to a runner's age. By middle age, all middle distances cease to exist entirely and become long distances.

mileage

any age over 40 when running a mile seems impossible.

1 METER

Mount Washington Race

milestones kidney ailment common among long-distance runners.

mistletoe nickname for a very fast runner.

moderation limiting your running to a sensible enough level so that it doesn't interfere with your eating, drinking, smoking and sex life.

momentum erroneous concept derived from Newtonian physics, which posits that a body in motion tends to stay in motion. In fact, when that body belongs to a runner, it stops for a variety of reasons, including blisters, a good-looking member of the opposite sex or simply because it's 42 years old and the first-run Monday night movie begins in 5 minutes.

Mount Washington Race uphill race held annually in New Hampshire on an 8-mile course that begins at the foot of Mount Washington and ends at the 6,288-foot summit. White-clad attendants wait at the finish line with nets to recapture the participants, put them back into their straitjackets and return them to their padded cells until the following year's competition.

muscle definition one of those lumpy fiber things under your skin that go to bones and joints and ligaments and tendons and things so you can run and jump and move and stuff.

muscle fatigue mental condition common to runners who spend time in summer beach-resort areas, consisting of extreme boredom with the same seafood dish served night after night.

N

naive	anyone who watches a marathon and says, "Hey! Those folks look like they're having fun!"
nagging knee injury	knee injury that causes one's spouse to say, "You haven't done the shopping in two weeks, the kids need new shoes, your mother has been here for a month and all you do is watch M*A*S*H reruns."
narcissist	marathon runner who, at the finish line, asks the medical team offering a mylar plastic reflection blanket to stand back five feet and hold the blanket by the corners.
natural	term applied to one's own running form. (See "*unnatural*")
NCAA	famous debating team that on running issues always takes the position opposite to an equally well-known team, the AAU.
1984 Summer Olympics	George Orwell's futuristic novel about a series of athletic events connected by freeways and beamed onto the homescreens of the citizenry, with periodic interruptions by heroes of the culture exhorting the viewers to buy beer, insurance and automobiles.
non-pros	(1) (Latin/legal—*v.*) To enter a *non prosequitor* against another party. (2) (track and field—*n.*) World-class

runners who have paid for their new cars, new homes, worldwide travel, entertainment and designer wardrobes by astute management of the money they made when they had a paper route in high school.

nostalgia

affectionate recollection of the period when you could still improve your personal best times.

nouveau riche

anyone who bought stock in a little-known Yugoslavian running-shoe company with a three-stripe logo in 1965 for one dinar a share.

numismatics

the collection of medals and coins, e.g., a first place at the Summer Olympics and the paid endorsements that follow.

obsessive

term applied to anyone who puts in more hours running than you do.

obsolete

the $300 running outfit you bought last spring.

odometer

device used in detecting the length of time the same sweat socks have been worn.

official timer	timing device used to ensure that officials at running competitions are paid only for the time that they are actually on the job.
optimal conditions	(for the serious runner) A slight wind, an overcast sky, cool weather and stiff competition. (for most runners) A tropical breeze, a bright moonlit night and an attractive, cooperative member of the opposite sex.
optimist	a 5-foot 2-inch, 240-pound runner who smokes two packs a day and decides on a strategy for running the Boston Marathon that includes making up for lost time on the Heartbreak Hill section.
ordeal	synonym for long-distance running. Other terms include suffering, misery, wretchedness, agony and despair.
organizer	individual who finances running competitions and supervises their details purely for the love of the sport, the thrill of competition and 75 percent of the gross.
orthopedic surgeon	medical specialist who is highly skilled in reducing the swelling in runners' bank accounts.
orthotics	prescription inserts for running shoes that have no effect on performance, but always assure an increase in the cost of the footwear by a factor of ten.
overtrained	term describing the anxious runner who, worried about the deteriorating condition of the country's railroad system, but even more afraid of flying, arranges travel

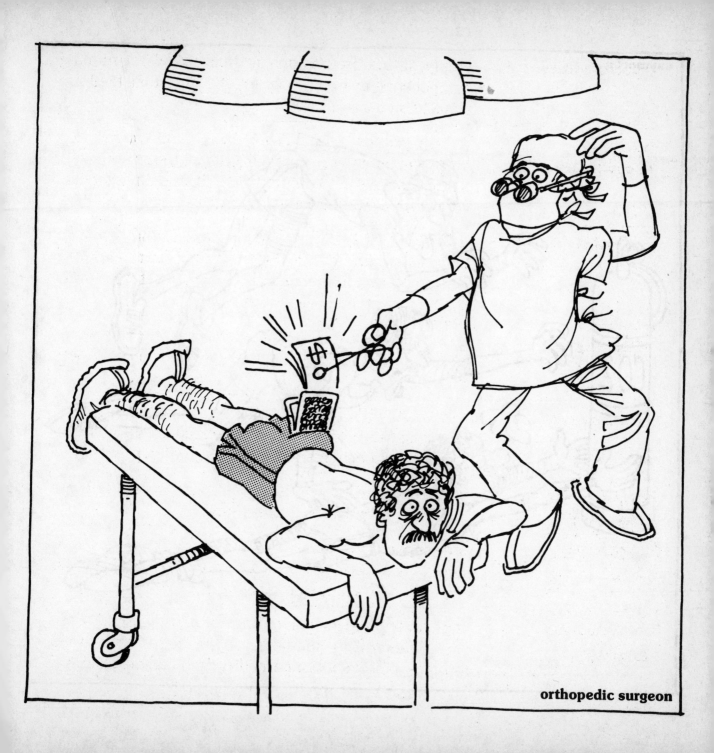

orthopedic surgeon

to a running event by making seventeen separate Amtrak reservations in the hopes that one of the trains will leave on time.

oxygen   gas involved in a complicated chemical process that runners have perfected to produce lactic acid. Runners go to extreme lengths to pass oxygen across the semi-permeable membrane of their lungs. It is then carried by hemoglobin in the red blood cells to the muscles, where it combines with lactose sugar, producing lactic acid. A much easier way to achieve the same result is to let a quart of milk sit outside the refrigerator overnight.

oxymoron   (1) Combination of contradictory or incongruous words, as "world-class amateur." (*See also "running for pleasure."*) (2) Runner who, at the end of an exhausting race, goes for the CO_2 bottle.

P

pace setter   runner who, without reference to his or her position in a race, is wearing Gucci jogging shoes, Yves Saint Laurent shorts and a Norma Kamali tank top.

pacing   walking up and down in your living room like a caged animal after your spouse, having been picked up by an astonishingly attractive member of the opposite sex, leaves the house saying, "Now, sweetie, if my running club decides to drive out to Heartthrob Mountain for our annual spring run, the whole group may just have to stay over at Honeymoon Lodge for the night. But don't worry, there's yesterday's leftover pizza in the freezer."

pack
(1) Standard deck of cards carried by all serious runners to out-of-town events, used in the evenings for poker, bridge and other card games in order to sharpen the mind for the running competition. (2) The players in such a card game. (3) (compound phrases) "Breaking away from the pack"—to leave such a card game for food, alcoholic beverages or in rare cases, because the running event is about to begin. "Ice pack"—arrangement of ice cubes around the alcoholic beverages served at such a card game. "Six pack"—the minimum unit of such alcoholic beverages required by participants in the card game.

pain
the basic unit of running. In the formula, $r \times t = p$ (where r stands for rate, t for time, and p for pain), increases in pain can be obtained either by increasing the rate (speed) of running or by increasing the time (duration). For those who are simply too out of shape to get their pain through running, approximately the same results can be obtained by pouring boiling water over the feet, sleeping on a seven- by three-ball array of bowling balls or snorting Ajax cleanser.

personal best

pants leg	last segment of a 10K race, so termed because of the type of breathing it induces.
peaking	(1) Reaching the top of one's abilities for a particular running event. (2) Reaching the top of the co-ed shower divider to see if that cute runner with the red tank top and shorts looks as good without them.
personal best	(1) (regarding oneself) A record that one will shortly improve on. (2) (regarding others) A lie, falsehood or distortion of the truth.
personal computer	any member of one's family who is willing to stand in the rain at the halfway mark of a marathon and shout, "You've done thirteen miles, one-hundred-seventy-two-and-a-half yards in two hours, thirty-seven minutes and fifty-nine seconds. You're right on pace."
Plain of Marathon	site of a battle in 490 B.C. between the Athenians and the Persians. News of the Athenian victory was carried from the battleground by a messenger named Pheiddipides who ran the 26 miles to Athens, gasped that the Athenians had won, then collapsed and died—presumably of overexertion—a short while later. A recently unearthed tablet recording the event tells of the actual cause of Pheiddipides' demise. He died of shock when, in reply to his gasped information, a bystander said, "We know. A messenger on a horse brought the news an hour-and-a-half ago, idiot!"

plantar warts	painful viral growths usually found on the soles of runner's feet, believed in medieval times to have been contracted as a result of jogging on one's toads.
plateau	a momentary leveling out of personal performance that is surpassed in a week by people in their twenties, in half a year by people in their thirties who make great sacrifices, and never by anyone over forty.
Pole vault	place where Polish Olympic track stars keep their money.
pronation	(1) A term coined 10 years ago by running-shoe manufacturers, which permits them to draw confusing pictures of the human foot in shoe advertisements. (2) An entire country of professional athletes for example, hockey players in the USSR "Overpronation"—secret satellite observation of such countries. "Anti-overpronation"—ground-to-air missiles designed to defend against such secret observation.
prostrate	prone position assumed by weekend runners at the end of their first organized competition. For older, out-of-shape runners, this position—which lasts longer and is more exaggerated—is called an "enlarged prostrate."
pulse check	the $60 check you give a doctor for taking your pulse and saying, "No, you didn't have a heart attack during your last 20K run, it's just gas. Take two Tums and call me in the morning."

prostrate

Q

quadriceps   muscle in the front of the thigh that you didn't know you had until you began to run uphill.

qualify   to meet the stringent demands of an organized running event, the most important of which is paying the entrance fee on time.

quartermaster   runner who excels both at the 440-yard dash and the arcade version of Pac-Man.

quattuordecillion   (1) Cardinal number represented by 1 followed by 45 zeros. (2) Perceived distance, in miles, to the end of a marathon by someone at the four-fifths mark.

R

rabbit   anyone who is ahead of you in a race.

race relations   sexual relationships between runners attending a race, particularly when they're away from home.

race walking   form of competitive walking, the object of which is to walk as quickly as possible for long distances while attempting to look like Charlie Chaplin. Race walking belongs to a special category of Olympic events for which style points are awarded for looking silly. Other events in this category include the hop-skip-jump, the hammer throw, and any form of weight lifting.

raison d'etre   (French) Runner's high-energy, dried-grape snack food (literally, "raisin to eat") developed by French vintners. Mexican grain growers mix these raisins with nuts and grains to make an even higher-energy mix called "gran-ola," Spanish for "grand hello."

relay   repetition of sexual relationships between runners attending a race, particularly when they're away from home.

Right Stuff, The   generic phrase for the runner who sports the very best running equipment including $400 hand-made running shoes; a designer training suit; ultra-light shirt and shorts; a Swiss chronometer; and a very attractive member of the opposite sex who, waiting at the finish line with a bottle of champagne, thinks sweat and dehydration are a turn on.

Road Runners Club of America   nationwide organization whose members collect and exchange memorabilia on every Wiley Coyote cartoon in existence. The secret RRCA greeting is "Meep meep!" The finish line of the annual RRCA picnic relay race is inevitably located at the edge of a mile-high canyon, and the batons passed from one team member to another are sticks of dynamite with lighted fuses.

Rob De Castella	phrase used by medieval Italian burglars who preyed on aristocrats, as in "First we rob de townhouse, den we rob de castella."
Royal Canadian Air Force Exercises	complete body-strengthening system for runners and other athletes that gradually works up to exercises involving 100 reps of carabou strafing, 200 reps of tundra buzzing and 2,000 reps of Moosehead beer drinking, this last accompanied by the phrase, "Git ahf, yuh hoser, an' git me another brew, hey?"
run amok	to jog behind pig pens, stables and barns.
run for office	(1) Enter into a contest for an elected position, usually by being photographed in jogging clothes—the current political symbols of health, honesty and family involvement. (2) Exercise in which the participant, fully clothed and late for work, has to sprint in order to jump onto some form of transportation.
runners	(psychoanal.) Individuals whose behavior tends toward asocial and masochistic activities and whose mental makeup is characterized by grandiose fantasies, hypochondria and a compulsion to expose their thinly-clad bodies to terrible weather.
runner's elbow	common ailment among long-distance runners resulting from bruising contact at the beginning of a race, the constant pumping motion required to sustain the pace, or fatigue in the elbow joint due to the constant bending required to consume alcoholic beverages.

running for pleasure

runner's knee	an effective defensive move used by a female runner when a menacing stranger jumps into her path, grabs her by the shoulders and says, "Let's get it on, Baby Cakes!"
running boom	sudden expansion of the U.S. economy due to extraordinary increases in the sales of ice bags, analgesic ointments, elastic bandages, leg braces and crutches.
running for pleasure	basic contradiction in terms. Other examples include: "a fun third-degree burn," "riotous root canal work," and "throwing up for laughs."
running form	Las Vegas publication giving odds on probable marathon winners: e.g., Alberto Salazar—2 to 1; Orson Welles—198,478,362 to 1.
running in place	a conditioning technique that *effectively* removes running's last barrier to total boredom.
running mate	(1) The spouse of a candidate for public office who is usually photographed with the candidate in running gear in order to promote the candidate's image as a healthy, lively person. (See *"run for office."*) (2) One of the most difficult and strenuous positions described in the *Kama Sutra*.
Running Revolution	the loosely knit, subversive organization of more than 185 million people in the United States who, against all urging, medical evidence and insults, refuse to run.
running scared	normal emotional condition of joggers who choose to get their exercise on roads used by motorcycle gangs.

seasoned runner

Running U.　(1) Any of several Sun-belt universities with extensive track programs. (2) Offhand phrase used by sports-shoe sales personnel, viz., "Oh, these'll be running you about $300, and I'll throw in the socks."

run-on sentence　a grammatical structure having two subjects and two verbs, used by spectators to encourage their friends in a marathon, as in, "Oh, Jane, see Dick run, run on, Dick, run on!"

run roughshod　to run in football cleats.

S

seasoned runner　(1) Term you use to describe yourself if you are over 40. (2) Term you use to describe anyone else of any age who can run faster and farther than you can.

second wind　the position behind the leader in playful sprints. (See "*fartlek.*")

shin splints　temporary wooden braces put on the legs of runners who decided to take up an easier sport like skiing, as they are carried off the hill by the ski patrol and taken to the emergency room.

shock absorption runner's ability to withstand bad news, for example, that the first prize for his or her last marathon win is an all-expenses-paid trip to Newark, New Jersey.

slapdash what you do when you are totally fed up with the runner next to you who keeps spitting on your shoes. Also called "hit-and-run."

speed work any running that immediately follows the ingestion or inhalation of "flash dancers," "crazy reds," "purple bombers," or "locker room lasers." The quarter-mile splits for such runners over a 2-mile course are, typically, (first mile) 49 seconds, 50 seconds, 51 seconds, 1/2 hour; (second mile) 2 hours, 5 hours, 17 hours, 2 days.

split time the time it takes for a runner doing warm-up exercises to stretch out the leg muscles by doing the splits. The following table gives average split times as a function of the runner's age.

Age (in years)	Split Time
5	1 sec.
15	4 sec.
25	30 sec.
35	1/2 hr.
45 +	never

spring referring to the degree of resilience in a runner's legs, the term is derived from the season of the same name

starter's gun

when runners of the opposite sex forget about chasing after improved times and chase after each other instead.

sprinter	painful sliver of wood injurious to Japanese runners using traditional wooden footwear, as in "Son-of-a-bonzai, this sprinter's kirring me!"
spurt	sudden burst of energy carrying a runner past a competitor, across the finish line or even off the course entirely for a beer, a cigarette and a good dinner. A more sustained spurt is called a "charge," which is typically directed toward establishments that accept Visa, Mastercharge or American Express.
stamina	speech impediment common to beginning runners, as in, "B-b-but you said we'd quit after h-h-half a m-m-mile!"
starter's gun	(1) Pistol loaded with blanks, used to start a race. (2) Pistol loaded with live ammunition used to encourage runners to start a race in extreme weather conditions.
starting blocks	phobias first described by Freud that prevent a person from starting a run, for example, "I'm going to have to wait until this blister goes down," or "You go ahead and I'll catch up when this damn leg cramp loosens up," or "I couldn't find my shoes."
stress fracture	a bone fracture common to executive joggers who trip over curbs because their minds are on yesterday's loss of a major client, $970,000 in overdue accounts receiv-

able and a memo from the president of the company saying, "See me on this immediately and you'd better have a damn good explanation!"

stretching exercises	making warm-up exercises last longer than normal so that actual running time is minimized. If warm-ups are stretched to 2 hours, for example, only 10 minutes of a marathon need be run.
sub-4-minute mile	a very poor performance for a modern submarine.
sweat	one of the four basic benefits of running first described by Winston Churchill, who also included in his list blood, toil and tears.
sweat bands	heavily costumed marching musicians who provide entertainment during tropical track events. The marchers face the ever-present danger of overexertion which can lead to a deficiency in the body's immune system, a syndrome termed "band aids."
sweat socks	blows delivered by irritated joggers to the heads of people who get in their way when jogging in August in Laredo, Texas.

T

tank top special protective garment worn by runners in Beirut. Comes complete with turret and swivel cannon.

tant pis (French) A canvas shelter manufactured in France, put up at marathons to house temporary toilet facilities.

Three Mile Island site of a 3-mile race in Pennsylvania run at night with no auxiliary lighting needed because the course glows in the dark.

timing sixth sense developed by weekend runners that allows them to return home from exercise just after the garbage has been taken out and just before lunch begins.

training suit warm-up suit for infant runners consisting of a bunny-print pullover and diapers that have struts and wheels angling out from the sides to provide balance and support.

triathletes advice given to those who feel they are not articulate enough to talk with stockbrokers or copywriters.

Trivial Pursuit an increasingly popular group game consisting of putting on jogging garb and running around the neighborhood for no apparent reason.

2K two kilometers (= 1.24 miles). Usually the first serious distance attempted by middle-aged executives who are trying to get back into shape. The abbreviation "2K" comes from an inverse association with K^2, the world's second highest mountain, which is what the distance looks like to these runners.

U

ultra-light	term applied to any running equipment that costs more than $75 an ounce.
ultra-marathon	a form of capital punishment ruled "cruel and unusual" by law courts, which accept the rack, drawing and quartering, and boiling in oil.
unnatural	term applied to anyone else's running form but your own. (See "*natural.*")
unsportsmanlike	what other runners are when they elbow you as you crowd them, step on your heels when you are in front of them, or don't move aside when you are behind them on a narrow track. (See "*competitive.*")
urine test	competition the night before a marathon in which runners loading up on liquid carbohydrates are judged for distance, accuracy and style.

V

vasoconstriction   restricted flow of blood in marathon runner's major blood vessels due to binding caused when shoes, crotch and armpits are jammed with too many gobs of vaseline.

vegetables   (1) Sources of vitamins, minerals, fiber and nutrients which are very important for a runner's diet. (2) General descriptive term for the condition of runners at the end of an ultra-marathon.

Venus de Milo   (Greek myth, literally "Venus of the Mile") Legendary female miler who is said to have increased her times dramatically by substantial reduction of upper body weight.

Verrazano— Narrows Bridge   site of an annual fall New York ritual wherein the entire population of Staten Island attempts to escape to Brooklyn simultaneously, and all of the escapees lose their sweat clothes in the process.

W

Wall, The   psychological barrier encountered by East German runners consisting of leaden legs, feelings of exhaustion and futility, and a 20-foot-high fence protected with razor wire and machine gun turrets.

warm-up exercises kissing; tossing down shots of brandy; standing close to a stove or fireplace; taking saunas and steambaths; soaking in a hot tub; and other similar activities used to avoid actually running. (See *"cool-down exercises."*)

warm-up suit an initial court action, usually preceding a more serious request for support, for example, Joanna Carson saying, "Your honor, all I want are the hand weights, the Walkman and Gatorade money."

weight-training training in patience that middle-aged marathoners give their families, who must stand at the finish line and wait and wait and wait.

wet weather basic excuse for not running. Other, related excuses include cold weather, hot weather and, in fact, any weather the mention of which won't be laughed at by one's peers. Warm, dry weather can be used as an excuse only by incorporating an auxiliary explanation such as a pollen count that one swears will induce a fatal asthma attack. Cool, dry weather requires even more creative inventions such as, "My doctor says I can't run today because it's too close to the autumnal equinox—something to do with tidal action and increased risk of pulmonary edema. I don't know, but he's the expert."

will power rigid self-discipline developed by runners who apply it to building up their cardiovascular systems and endur-

weight-training

ance so as to outlive other relatives who are also named in the family will.

wimp (Swahili) Term used by runners from Kenya to describe a competitor who wears shoes and gets short of breath running up Foot Rip Mountain's 50K goat track.

winded beginning of a question gasped by a middle-aged individual who takes up running after a 22-year layoff and clocks a 15-minute mile. The rest of the question is, " . . . they change this jogging track so that it always goes uphill?"

winter sports jolly, hearty individuals who actually think it's fun to run in sub-zero temperatures.

world-class runner any member of a select group of athletes who make commercials for American Express.

x-rays diagnostic pictures about which an orthopedic surgeon says, "I can't tell a damn thing from these. That'll be $500."

Y

yard (1) Distance by which you beat Alberto Salazar in the Olympic Marathon, just before you wake up and remember you went to bed with your Nikes on. (2) Grassy area surrounding suburban dwellings that simply cannot be mowed or raked at the moment because of the overwhelming need to join your sexy blond neighbor in a jog around the neighborhood.

Z

zealot (1) Fanatic. (2) One who says to an extraordinarily attractive, willing member of the opposite sex, "Look, I'm going to have to take a rain-check on the passion fruit body oil rub until after I've done my 10K run."

zephyr any wind that is at a runner's back. (See *"gale."*)